"It's hard to connect with your child without first... As counselors and speakers at parenting events across the country, we spend a great deal of time teaching parents about development. To know *where* your child is—not just physically, but emotionally, socially, and spiritually, helps you to truly know and understand *who* your child is. And that understanding is the key to connecting. The Phase Guides give you the tools to do just that. Our wise friends Reggie and Kristen have put together an insightful, hopeful, practical, and literal year-by-year guide that will help you to understand and connect with your child at every age."

SISSY GOFF
M.ED., LPC-MHSP, DIRECTOR OF CHILD & ADOLESCENT COUNSELING AT DAYSTAR COUNSELING MINISTRIES IN NASHVILLE, TENNESSEE, SPEAKER AND AUTHOR OF ARE MY KIDS ON TRACK?

"These resources for parents are fantastically empowering, absolute in their simplicity, and completely doable in every way. The hard work that has gone into the Phase Project will echo through the next generation of children in powerful ways."

JENNIFER WALKER
RN BSN, AUTHOR AND FOUNDER OF MOMS ON CALL

"We all know where we want to end up in our parenting, but how to get there can seem like an unsolved mystery. Through the Phase Project series, Reggie Joiner and Kristen Ivy team up to help us out. The result is a resource that guides us through the different seasons of raising children, and provides a road map to parenting in such a way that we finish up with very few regrets."

SANDRA STANLEY
FOSTER CARE ADVOCATE, BLOGGER, WIFE TO ANDY STANLEY, MOTHER OF THREE

"Not only are the Phase Guides the most creative and well-thought-out guides to parenting I have ever encountered, these books are ESSENTIAL to my daily parenting. With a 13-year-old, 11-year-old, and 9-year-old at home, I am swimming in their wake of daily drama and delicacy. These books are a reminder to enjoy every second. Because it's just a phase."

CARLOS WHITTAKER
AUTHOR, SPEAKER, FATHER OF THREE

"As the founder of Minnie's Food Pantry, I see thousands of people each month with children who will benefit from the advice, guidance, and nuggets of information on how to celebrate and understand the phases of their child's life. Too often we feel like we're losing our mind when sweet little Johnny starts to change his behavior into a person we do not know. I can't wait to start implementing the principles of these books with my clients to remind them . . . it's just a phase."

CHERYL JACKSON
FOUNDER OF MINNIE'S FOOD PANTRY, AWARD-WINNING PHILANTHROPIST, AND GRANDMOTHER

"I began exploring this resource with my counselor hat on, thinking how valuable this will be for the many parents I spend time with in my office. I ended up taking my counselor hat off and putting on my parent hat. Then I kept thinking about friends who are teachers, coaches, youth pastors, and children's ministers, who would want this in their hands. What a valuable resource the Orange team has given us to better understand and care for the kids and adolescents we love. I look forward to sharing it broadly."

DAVID THOMAS
LMSW, DIRECTOR OF FAMILY COUNSELING, DAYSTAR COUNSELING MINISTRIES, SPEAKER AND AUTHOR OF ARE MY KIDS ON TRACK? AND WILD THINGS: THE ART OF NURTURING BOYS

"I have always wished someone would hand me a manual for parenting. Well, the Phase Guides are more than what I wished for. They guide, inspire, and challenge me as a parent—while giving me incredible insight into my children at each age and phase. Our family will be using these every year!"

COURTNEY DEFEO
AUTHOR OF IN THIS HOUSE, WE WILL GIGGLE, MOTHER OF TWO

"As I speak to high school students and their parents, I always wonder to myself: What would it have been like if they had better seen what was coming next? What if they had a guide that would tell them what to expect and how to be ready? What if they could anticipate what is predictable about the high school years before they actually hit? These Phase Guides give a parent that kind of preparation so they can have a plan when they need it most."

JOSH SHIPP
AUTHOR, TEEN EXPERT, AND YOUTH SPEAKER

"The Phase Guides are incredibly creative, well researched, and filled with inspirational actions for everyday life. Each age-specific guide is catalytic for equipping parents to lead and love their kids as they grow up. I'm blown away and deeply encouraged by the content and by its creators. I highly recommend Phase resources for all parents, teachers, and influencers of children. This is the stuff that challenges us and changes our world. Get them. Read them. And use them!"

DANIELLE STRICKLAND
OFFICER WITH THE SALVATION ARMY, AUTHOR, SPEAKER, MOTHER OF TWO

"It's true that parenting is one of life's greatest joys but it is not without its challenges. If we're honest, parenting can sometimes feel like trying to choreograph a dance to an ever-changing beat. It can be clumsy and riddled with well-meaning missteps. If parenting is a dance, this Parenting Guide is a skilled instructor refining your technique and helping you move gracefully to a steady beat. For those of us who love to plan ahead, this guide will help you anticipate what's to come so you can be poised and ready to embrace the moments you want to enjoy."

TINA NAIDOO
MSSW, LCSW EXECUTIVE DIRECTOR, THE POTTER'S HOUSE OF DALLAS, INC.

PARENTING YOUR NEW BABY

A GUIDE TO MAKING THE MOST OF THE "I NEED YOU NOW" PHASE

KRISTEN IVY AND REGGIE JOINER

PARENTING YOUR NEW BABY
A GUIDE TO MAKING THE MOST OF THE
"I NEED YOU NOW" PHASE

Published by Orange, a division of The reThink Group, Inc.,
5870 Charlotte Lane, Suite 300,
Cumming, GA 30040 U.S.A.

©2017 The Phase Project
Authors: Kristen Ivy and Reggie Joiner
Lead Editor: Karen Wilson
Editing Team: Melanie Williams, Hannah Crosby, Sherry Surratt

Art Direction: Ryan Boon and Hannah Crosby
Book Design: FiveStone and Sharon van Rossum
Project Manager : Nate Brandt

Printed in the United States of America
First Edition 2017
17 18 19 20 21 22 23 24 25 26

07/2020

Special thanks to:

Jim Burns, Ph.D for guidance and consultation on having conversations about sexual integrity

Jon Acuff for guidance and consultation on having conversations about technological responsibility

Jean Sumner, MD for guidance and consultation on having conversations about healthy habits

Every educator, counselor, community leader, and researcher who invested in the Phase Project

TABLE OF CONTENTS

HOW TO USE THIS GUIDE .... pg. 9

WELCOME TO A NEW PHASE .... pg. 10

52 WEEKS
TO PARENT YOUR NEW BABY .... pg. 13

pg. 14 **MEASURE YOUR WEEKS**   pg. 22 **DISCOVER THIS PHASE**

SIX THINGS
EVERY KID NEEDS .... pg. 31

pg. 34 **LOVE**   pg. 52 **FUN**
ONE QUESTION YOUR   WAYS TO HAVE FUN
BABY IS ASKING   WITH YOUR BABY

pg. 40 **STORIES**   pg. 58 **TRIBES**
BOOKS TO READ   ADULTS WHO MIGHT INFLUENCE
TO YOUR BABY   YOUR BABY

pg. 46 **WORK**   pg. 64 **WORDS**
WORK YOUR   WORDS YOUR BABY
BABY CAN DO   NEEDS TO HEAR

FOUR CONVERSATIONS
TO HAVE IN THIS PHASE .... pg. 71

pg. 74 **HEALTH**   pg. 86 **TECHNOLOGY**
ESTABLISH BASIC NUTRITION   ENJOY THE ADVANTAGES

pg. 80 **SEX**   pg. 92 **FAITH**
INTRODUCE THEM   INCITE THEIR SENSE
TO THEIR BODY   OF WONDER

THE RHYTHM OF YOUR WEEK .... pg. 98

PHASE LIFE MAP OVERVIEW .... pg. 106

HOW TO USE THIS ~~BOOK~~ ~~JOURNAL~~ GUIDE

The guide you hold in your hand doesn't have very many words, but it does have a lot of ideas. Some of these ideas come from thousands of hours of research. Others come from parents, educators, and volunteers who spend every day with kids the same age as yours. This guide won't tell you everything about your kid, but it will tell you a few things about kids at this age.

The best way to use this guide is to take what these pages tell you about babies and combine it with what you know is true about your baby.

Let's sum it up:

**THINGS ABOUT BABIES +
THOUGHTS ABOUT *YOUR* BABY =
YOUR GUIDE TO THE NEXT 52 WEEKS OF PARENTING**

After each idea in this guide, there are pages with a few questions designed to prompt you to think about your kid, your family, and yourself as a parent. The only guarantee we give to parents who use this guide is this: You will mess up some things as a parent this year. Actually, that's a guarantee to every parent, regardless. But you, you picked up this book! You want to be a better parent. And that's what we hope this guide will do: help you parent your baby just a little better, simply because you paused to consider a few ideas that can help you make the most of this phase.

THE NEW BABY PHASE

Regardless of how many friends, family members, and perfect strangers try to paint an accurate picture of parenthood, there's nothing anyone can say that adequately prepares you for that heart-stretching moment you hold your newborn for the very first time.

And the sentiments only grow exponentially from there. There aren't words in any language capable of conveying the myriad of emotions you will experience as a new parent. Love. Gratitude. Exhaustion. Fear. Joy. Frustration. Excitement. Hate.

(Okay, you won't *really* hate your baby, just the sound of your baby crying at three in the morning when it's only been half an hour since her last feeding.)

Maybe that's the best word to describe the new baby phase: *emotional*. It's emotional for you. It's emotional for them. But despite the crying—both yours and theirs—there is something indescribably wonderful about that first year of life.

Somewhere along the way, in the delirium of teething and feedings and diapers and sleep schedules, something almost magical takes place.

It's in the way your baby smells after a bath, wrapped in a towel and laying on your chest. It's in the way their eyelids flutter when they sleep. It's in the shape of their perfect little mouths, the length of their tiny fingernails, and the velvety feel of their skin against yours. There's something alluring about the way that they are totally and completely brand new.

In my work as a preschool director, my favorite rooms to visit were the ones assigned to this age group. These were my volunteers' favorite rooms, too. People literally wait in line to hold a baby. To rock a baby. To ooooh and ahhhh over baby's impossibly long eyelashes or new hairbow.

There is a great sense of promise that adds to the allure of this age. Literally, anything is possible. The pages of their story are gleamingly blank, striking with potential.

As a parent, you have many phases ahead, and each one has its own set of unique possibilities. But right here, right now, you have something you will never have again—at least not in this way. You could think about it like this: You will never have messed up less as a parent than you have at this moment. Really. This is the beginning. You have a fresh start. And even though it's scary, even though you don't know what you're doing (none of us do), you have everything you need—*you*.

That's right. Because, despite the thousands of mass-market baby products available, there is only one thing your baby really needs right now—your baby needs you.

Some days it may seem like they need you a little too much, or a little too often, or a little too immediately. Don't worry. With every passing month, they will discover a new ability that lets them need you a little less.

But for now, in this fleeting new baby phase, they need you. And you are enough.

- HOLLY CRAWSHAW
PRESCHOOL DIRECTOR, EDUCATOR, & AUTHOR

52
WEEKS
—
TO PARENT YOUR
NEW BABY

WHEN YOU SEE
HOW MUCH

Time

YOU HAVE LEFT

—

YOU TEND TO DO

More

WITH THE TIME
YOU HAVE NOW.

THERE ARE APPROXIMATELY
936 WEEKS
FROM THE TIME A BABY IS BORN UNTIL THEY GROW UP AND MOVE TO WHATEVER IS NEXT.

Right now, that might seem like a lot of weeks. The future probably still feels far away and full of possibility. But the truth is your baby will grow up faster than you ever dreamed.

That's why every week counts. Of course, each week might not feel significant. There may be weeks in your baby's first year when all you really accomplish is feeding them. That's okay.

Take a deep breath.
You don't have to get everything done this week.

But what happens in your child's life week after week, year after year, adds up over time. So, it just might be a good idea to put a number to your weeks.

MEASURE IT OUT.

How many weeks do you have with your kid until they graduate and move to whatever is next? Write down the number.

HINT: If you want a little help counting it out, you can download the free Parent Cue app on all mobile platforms.

_____

_____

_____

_____

CREATE A VISUAL COUNTDOWN.

Find a jar and fill it with one marble for each week you have remaining with your child. Then make a habit of removing one marble every week as a reminder to make the most of your time you have with your child.

Where can you place your visual countdown so you will see it frequently?

_____

_____

_____

_____

Which day of the week is best for you to remove a marble?

_____

_____

_____

Is there anything you want to do each week as you remove a marble? (Examples: *say a prayer, write in a baby book, retell one favorite memory from this past week*)

_____

_____

_____

_____

_____

_____

_____

_____

_____

_____

_____

_____

EVERY PHASE IS A

TIMEFRAME

IN A KID'S LIFE

WHEN YOU CAN

LEVERAGE

DISTINCTIVE

OPPORTUNITIES

TO INFLUENCE

THEIR

future.

YOU ONLY HAVE
52 WEEKS
WITH YOUR NEW BABY

while they are still a baby.

Then they will be a toddler,

and you will never know them as a baby again.

That might be incredibly emotional,

or it might be the best news you've heard all day.

Or to say it another way:

Before you know it, your baby will grow up a little more and . . .

sleep through the night.

play independently.

learn to tell you what's wrong.

Just remember, the phase you are in now has remarkable potential. Before their first birthday, there are some distinctive opportunities you don't want to miss. So, as you count down the next 52 weeks, pay attention to what makes these weeks different from the rest of the weeks you will have with your child as they grow.

What are some things you have noticed about your baby in this phase that you really enjoy?

_____

_____

_____

_____

_____

_____

_____

_____

_____

_____

_____

_____

_____

_____

_____

_____

_____

_____

_____

_____

_____

What is something new you are learning as a parent during this phase?

_____

_____

_____

_____

_____

_____

_____

_____

_____

_____

_____

_____

_____

_____

_____

_____

_____

_____

_____

_____

NEW BABY

—

THE PHASE WHEN NOBODY SLEEPS, EVERYBODY SMELLS, AND ONE MESMERIZING BABY CONVINCES YOU,

"I need you now."

YOU'VE NEVER KNOWN SLEEP DEPRIVATION LIKE THIS.

Maybe that's why every book on babies seems to be primarily dedicated to keeping them happy (stop the crying, please!) or helping them sleep longer (so you can sleep longer).

YOU'VE NEVER REALLY SMELLED LIKE THIS.

When faced with the choice between sleep or a shower, there are days (no one's counting how many) when cleanliness doesn't win out. The smells aren't all bad though. Just watch how long it takes grandma to lean over and sniff a new baby the first time they meet.

YOU'VE NEVER BEEN NEEDED LIKE THIS.

Your baby needs you more desperately, more consistently, and more frequently than at any other stage of life. They need you to feed them, clean up their messes, and help them get to sleep. They need you to comfort them, smile at them, and entertain them. And although the days are long and the tasks can feel demanding, only one thing matters most at this phase—you show up.

THIS
YEAR
YOUR
BABY
IS
changing.

PHYSICALLY

- Lifts their head and chest (3-4 months)
- Reaches for objects & rolls over (4-6 months)
- Sits up & grabs with two fingers (6-8 months)
- Crawls (6-10 months)
- Stands unsupported & maybe even walks (11-12 months)

VERBALLY

- Has distinctive cries for different needs (0-6 weeks)
- Turns toward your voice (3 months)
- Mimics your tone and "babbles" (6 months)
- Understands a few simple words (9 months)
- Understands around 70 words & may say first "words" (12 months)

MENTALLY

- Is mildly aware of everything
- Learns through their five senses

EMOTIONALLY

- Mirrors your expressions (2 months)
- Distinguishes happy faces from sad faces (4 months)
- Turns away from strangers to show fear (6 months)
- Shows surprise at loud noises (7 months)

What are some changes you are noticing in your baby?

_____

_____

_____

_____

_____

_____

_____

You may disagree with some of the characteristics we've shared about babies. That's because every baby is unique. What makes your baby different from babies in general?

_____

_____

_____

_____

_____

_____

_____

_____

What do you want to remember about your baby's first year?

Mark this page. Throughout the year, write down a few simple things you don't want to forget. If you want to be really thorough, there are about 52 blank lines. But some weeks, your best memory might be that nap you took instead of writing in this journal. That's okay.

_____

_____

_____

_____

_____

_____

_____

_____

_____

_____

_____

_____

_____

_____

_____

_____

_____

_____

_____

_____

_____

_____

_____

_____

_____

_____

_____

_____

_____

_____

_____

_____

_____

_____

_____

_____

_____

_____

_____

_____

_____

SIX THINGS
—

EVERY KID
NEEDS

YOUR KID **NEEDS** **6** **THINGS** OVER TIME

LOVE

STORIES

WORDS

WORK

TRIBES

FUN

OVER THE NEXT 936 WEEKS, YOUR CHILD WILL NEED MANY THINGS.

Some of the things your kid needs will change from phase to phase, but there are six things that every kid needs at every phase. In fact, these things may be the most important things you give your kid—other than food. Kids need food.

EVERY KID, AT EVERY PHASE, NEEDS . . .

LOVE
to give them a
sense of WORTH.

STORIES
to give them a bigger
PERSPECTIVE.

WORK
to give them
SIGNIFICANCE.

FUN
to give them
CONNECTION.

TRIBES
to give them
BELONGING.

WORDS
to give them
DIRECTION.

The next few pages are designed to help you think about how you will give your baby these six things, right now—before they turn one.

EVERY KID

NEEDS

love

OVER TIME

—

TO GIVE THEM

A SENSE OF

worth.

ONE QUESTION
YOUR BABY IS ASKING

Your baby has suddenly arrived in a world where . . .

no one speaks their language.

they are unsure how to coordinate their movements.

they have limited control over their next meal, next bath,

or next nap.

Your baby is asking one major question:

"AM I SAFE?"

As the parent of a baby who may cry more than you imagined, or sleep less than you had hoped, or poop more than you thought possible, your role may feel overwhelming at times. But remember this—in order to give your baby the love they need in this phase, you need to do one thing:

EMBRACE their physical needs.

The way you show up hour after hour, day after day, to feed, change, and soothe your baby is establishing a foundation of trust that will follow them for the rest of their life.

You are probably doing more than you realize to show your baby just how much you love them. Write down the schedule for a typical day that you might spend with your baby. Make a list of what you do for your baby and how much time it takes.

You may need to look at this list on a bad day to remember what a great parent you are.

_____

_____

_____

_____

_____

_____

_____

_____

_____

_____

_____

_____

_____

_____

_____

_____

_____

Showing love requires paying attention to what someone likes.
What does your baby seem to enjoy the most right now?

_____

_____

_____

_____

_____

_____

_____

_____

_____

_____

_____

_____

_____

_____

_____

_____

_____

_____

_____

_____

_____

_____

It's impossible to love anyone with the relentless effort a baby demands unless you have a little time for yourself. What can you do to refuel each week so you are able to give your baby the love they need?

_____

_____

_____

_____

_____

_____

_____

_____

_____

_____

_____

_____

_____

_____

_____

_____

_____

Who do you have around you supporting you this year?

EVERY KID

NEEDS

stories

OVER TIME

—

TO GIVE THEM

A BIGGER

perspective.

BOOKS TO READ
TO YOUR BABY

GIRAFFES CAN'T DANCE: TOUCH AND FEEL
by Giles Andreae

BARNYARD DANCE!
by Sandra Boynton

DEAR ZOO: A LIFT-THE-FLAP BOOK
by Rod Campbell

THE VERY HUNGRY CATERPILLAR
by Eric Carle

TIME FOR BED
by Mem Fox

BLACK ON WHITE
by Tana Hoban

SLEEPYHEADS
by Sandra J. Howatt

WHERE IS BABY'S BELLY BUTTON?
by Karen Katz

PAT THE BUNNY
by Dorothy Kunhardt

BROWN BEAR, BROWN BEAR, WHAT DO YOU SEE?
by Bill Martin Jr.
illustrated by Eric Carle

CHICKA CHICKA BOOM BOOM
by Bill Martin Jr.

FIRST 100 WORDS
by Roger Priddy

NUMBERS COLORS SHAPES
by Roger Priddy

GOOD NIGHT, GORILLA
by Peggy Rathmann

DR. SEUSS'S ABC
by Dr. Seuss

THAT'S NOT MY DINOSAUR
by Fiona Watt

BABY CAKES
by Karma Wilson

GOODNIGHT MOON
by Margaret Wise Brown

Kids need the kind of stories you will read to them over time. But they also need family stories. What can you do this year to capture your family's story so you can retell the story of this year to your child when they are older?

_____

_____

_____

_____

_____

_____

_____

_____

_____

_____

_____

_____

_____

_____

_____

_____

What makes your family history unique? How can you preserve
the story of your family's history for your child?

_____

_____

_____

_____

_____

_____

_____

_____

_____

_____

_____

_____

_____

_____

_____

_____

_____

_____

_____

_____

Are there other stories that matter to you? What are they, and how will you make them a part of the first 52 weeks of your baby's life?

_____

_____

_____

_____

_____

_____

_____

_____

_____

_____

_____

_____

_____

_____

_____

_____

_____

_____

_____

_____

_____

EVERY KID

NEEDS

work

OVER TIME

—

TO GIVE

THEM

significance.

WORK YOUR
BABY CAN DO

FOLLOW MOVING OBJECTS WITH THEIR EYES
(2-4 months)

HOLD THEIR HEAD UP
(tummy time, 3-4 months)

REACH, GRASP, AND HOLD ON
(4-6 months)

ROLL OVER
(4-6 months)

SIT UP
(6-8 month)

CRAWL
(6-10 months)

PULL UP ON FURNITURE
(9-10 months)

CLAP THEIR HANDS
(8-10 months)

STAND UP
(11-12 months)

POINT
(9-12 months)

TAKE A FIRST STEP
(12-15 months)

What are some things your baby has worked to accomplish so far?

_____

_____

_____

_____

_____

_____

_____

_____

_____

_____

_____

_____

_____

_____

_____

_____

_____

_____

_____

_____

_____

_____

How are you holding back to give your baby the space they need in order to do things on their own? And how do you reward their efforts?

_____

_____

_____

_____

_____

_____

_____

_____

_____

_____

_____

_____

_____

_____

_____

_____

_____

_____

_____

_____

What are things you hope your baby will be able to do independently in the next phase?

_____

_____

_____

_____

_____

_____

_____

_____

_____

_____

_____

_____

_____

_____

_____

_____

_____

_____

_____

How are you helping them develop those skills now?

_____

_____

_____

_____

_____

_____

_____

_____

_____

_____

_____

_____

_____

_____

_____

_____

_____

_____

_____

_____

_____

_____

EVERY KID

NEEDS

fun

OVER TIME

—

TO GIVE

THEM

connection.

WAYS TO HAVE FUN WITH YOUR BABY

TOYS:

MOBILES AND BOUNCY SEATS
(1-6 months)

PLAY MATS OR BLANKETS WITH INTERESTING TEXTURES
(1-12 months)

PLUSH TOYS AND TEDDY BEARS
(3-12 months)

RATTLES AND PLASTIC KEY RINGS
(3-12 months)

ANYTHING THAT PLAYS MUSIC
(3-12 months)

AN EXERSAUCER
(5-12 months)

STACKING RINGS
(12 months)

SHAPE SORTERS
(12 months)

BIG BLOCKS
(12 months)

ANYTHING WITH A MIRROR
(4 months-forever)

ACTIVITIES:

PEEK-A-BOO

SILLY NOISES

CRAZY FACES

DROP IT / PICK IT UP

FINGER PUPPETS

PASSING OBJECTS BACK AND FORTH

NAMING OPPOSITES

What are some activities that make you and your baby laugh?

When are the best times of the day, or week, for you to set aside to have fun with your baby?

_____

_____

_____

_____

_____

_____

_____

_____

_____

_____

_____

_____

_____

_____

_____

_____

_____

_____

This year, your baby will have some important celebrations. What are some ways you want to have fun on these special days?

1ST BIRTHDAY

_____

_____

_____

_____

_____

_____

_____

_____

_____

_____

_____

_____

_____

_____

_____

_____

_____

HOLIDAYS

_____

_____

_____

_____

_____

_____

_____

_____

_____

_____

_____

_____

_____

_____

_____

_____

_____

_____

_____

_____

_____

_____

EVERY KID

NEEDS

tribes

OVER TIME

—

TO GIVE

THEM

belonging.

ADULTS WHO MIGHT INFLUENCE YOUR BABY

PARENTS

PARENT'S FRIENDS

GRANDPARENTS

NURSERY WORKERS

AUNTS AND UNCLES

BABYSITTERS OR NANNIES

List at least five adults who have influence in your baby's life right now.

🔑 HINT: They're probably the adults your baby reaches for and doesn't shy away from.

_____

_____

_____

_____

_____

_____

_____

_____

_____

_____

_____

_____

_____

_____

_____

_____

_____

_____

What is one way these adults could help you and your baby this year?

EXAMPLES: pray for you, bring a meal, maybe even hold the baby while you get some sleep

_____

_____

_____

_____

_____

_____

_____

_____

_____

_____

_____

_____

_____

_____

_____

_____

_____

What are a few ways you could show these adults appreciation for the significant role they play in your child's life?

_____

_____

_____

_____

_____

_____

_____

_____

_____

_____

_____

_____

_____

_____

_____

_____

_____

_____

_____

_____

_____

_____

_____

_____

_____

_____

_____

_____

_____

_____

_____

_____

_____

_____

_____

_____

_____

_____

_____

_____

_____

_____

EVERY KID

NEEDS

words

OVER TIME

—

TO GIVE

THEM

direction.

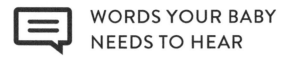

WORDS YOUR BABY NEEDS TO HEAR

Improving your child's vocabulary will help them in the phases to come. Here are a few ways you can help:

1.	**2.**	**3.**	**4.**	**5.**
Talk to your baby—the more, the better.	Speak slowly and clearly.	Make eye contact.	Point at objects when you name them.	Repeat the same word *a lot*.

What word (or words) describe your hopes for your child in this phase?

DETERMINED	MOTIVATED	GENTLE
ENCOURAGING	INTROSPECTIVE	PASSIONATE
SELF-ASSURED	ENTHUSIASTIC	PATIENT
ASSERTIVE	JOYFUL	FORGIVING
DARING	ENTERTAINING	CREATIVE
INSIGHTFUL	INDEPENDENT	WITTY
COMPASSIONATE	OBSERVANT	AMBITIOUS
AMIABLE	SENSITIVE	HELPFUL
EASY-GOING	ENDEARING	AUTHENTIC
DILIGENT	ADVENTUROUS	INVENTIVE
PROACTIVE	HONEST	DEVOTED
OPTIMISTIC	CURIOUS	GENUINE
FEARLESS	DEPENDABLE	ATTENTIVE
AFFECTIONATE	GENEROUS	HARMONIOUS
COURAGEOUS	COMMITTED	EMPATHETIC
CAUTIOUS	RESPONSIBLE	COURAGEOUS
DEVOTED	TRUSTWORTHY	FLEXIBLE
INQUISITIVE	THOUGHTFUL	CAREFUL
PATIENT	LOYAL	NURTURING
OPEN-MINDED	KIND	RELIABLE

Where can you place those words in your home so they will remind you what you want for your child this year?

_____

_____

_____

_____

_____

_____

_____

_____

_____

_____

_____

_____

_____

_____

_____

_____

_____

_____

_____

_____

_____

Babies understand approximately 70 words by their first birthday. What are some of the first words you hope your baby hears and understand?

_____

_____

_____

_____

_____

_____

_____

_____

_____

_____

_____

_____

_____

_____

_____

_____

_____

_____

FOUR
CONVERSATIONS
—

TO HAVE IN THIS
PHASE

WHEN YOU KNOW
WHERE YOU WANT
TO GO,

AND YOU KNOW
WHERE YOU ARE
NOW,

YOU CAN ALWAYS
DO SOMETHING

TO MOVE IN A
BETTER DIRECTION.

OVER THE 936 WEEKS OF YOUR CHILD'S LIFE, SOME CONVERSATIONS MAY MATTER MORE THAN OTHERS.

WHAT YOU SAY, FOR EXAMPLE, REGARDING . . .

Pirates

Spiders

and Football

MIGHT HAVE LESS IMPACT ON THEIR FUTURE THAN WHAT YOU SAY REGARDING . . .

Health

Sex

Technology

or Faith.

The next pages are about the conversations that matter most. On the left page is a destination—what you might want to be true in your kid's life 936 weeks from now. On the right page is a goal for conversations with your baby and a few suggestions about what you might want to say.

Healthy habits

—

LEARNING TO STRENGTHEN MY BODY THROUGH EXERCISE, NUTRITION, AND SELF-ADVOCACY

THIS YEAR YOU WILL

ESTABLISH BASIC NUTRITION

SO YOUR CHILD WILL HAVE CONSISTENT CARE AND EXPERIENCE A VARIETY OF FOOD.

You may not have conversations with your baby regarding healthy habits in this phase, but you will talk with someone about your child's health.

SAY THINGS LIKE . . .

HEY MOM, DO YOU KNOW OUR FAMILY MEDICAL HISTORY?
(Ask grandparents and relatives for a health history.)

HOW DO I KNOW IF HE'S GETTING ENOUGH TO EAT?
(Decide where you will go to get good advice about your baby's health.)

WHEN SHOULD WE SCHEDULE OUR NEXT APPOINTMENTS?
(Prioritize well visits with your pediatrician at 1, 2, 4, 6, 9, and 12 months.)

What are your goals for providing your baby with good nutrition and exercise? *(Okay, "exercise" may be a stretch, but tummy-time counts.)*

_____

_____

_____

_____

_____

_____

_____

_____

_____

_____

_____

_____

_____

_____

_____

_____

_____

Who will help you monitor and improve your baby's health?

What are your own health goals for this year? How can you improve the habits in your own life—*even in a phase when your most common health question might be, "Should I use their nap time to sleep or shower or eat?"*

_____

_____

_____

_____

_____

_____

_____

_____

_____

_____

_____

_____

_____

_____

_____

_____

_____

_____

_____

_____

_____
_____
_____
_____
_____
_____
_____
_____
_____
_____
_____
_____
_____
_____
_____
_____
_____
_____
_____
_____
_____
_____
_____
_____

Sexual integrity

—

GUARDING MY

POTENTIAL FOR

INTIMACY THROUGH

APPROPRIATE

BOUNDARIES

AND MUTUAL

RESPECT

THIS YEAR YOU WILL

INTRODUCE THEM TO THEIR BODY

**SO YOUR CHILD WILL DISCOVER THEIR BODY
AND DEFINE PRIVACY.**

Your conversations with your child regarding sexual integrity will never be simpler than they are right now. But it's never too early to start with some of the right words.

SAY THINGS LIKE . . .

GOD MADE YOUR
STRONG LITTLE LEGS.

GOD MADE
YOUR ELBOWS.

GOD MADE YOUR
VAGINA / PENIS.

(Use correct names of body parts as you bathe and change your child—experts suggest that learning proper words can protect your kid from potential harm as well as create a positive view of their body.)

What influences shaped your views of sex growing up? *(parents, media, friends, other adults . . .)*

_____

_____

_____

_____

_____

_____

_____

_____

_____

_____

_____

_____

_____

_____

_____

_____

_____

_____

_____

_____

_____

_____

_____

How does your own life story shape your future hopes for your child in this area?

_____

_____

_____

_____

_____

_____

_____

_____

_____

_____

_____

_____

_____

_____

_____

_____

_____

_____

When it comes to your child's sexuality, what do you hope is true for them 936 weeks from now?

_____

_____

_____

_____

_____

_____

_____

_____

_____

_____

_____

_____

_____

_____

_____

_____

_____

_____

_____

_____

Are you and your spouse, or your child's other parent, on the same page when it comes to talking about sex with your child? How might you work on a plan to communicate your hopes, expectations, and real-time conversations with your child about sex?

_____

_____

_____

_____

_____

_____

_____

_____

_____

_____

_____

_____

_____

_____

_____

_____

_____

Technological responsibility

—

LEVERAGING THE
POTENTIAL OF ONLINE
EXPERIENCES TO
ENHANCE MY OFFLINE
COMMUNITY
AND SUCCESS

THIS YEAR YOU WILL

ENJOY THE ADVANTAGES

SO YOUR CHILD WILL EXPERIENCE BOUNDARIES
AND HAVE POSITIVE EXPOSURE.

In spite of the research that warns you to absolutely never allow
your baby to make eye contact with a screen, technology has some
incredible benefits for you and your baby. Practically speaking, it's not
too soon to begin asking yourself a few questions about technology.

SAY THINGS LIKE . . .

**DOES IT REALLY MATTER IF
I FORGOT TO RECORD THE
LAST FEEDING IN THE APP?**
(Answer: No. As long as the baby
ate, she does not care.)

**IS THERE ANYONE OUT
THERE WHO CAN RELATE?**
(Use technology to connect to
other adults.)

LOOK AT THIS BABY!
(Take as many photos as you like.
You will enjoy seeing them later.)

What kind of digital access was available to you when you were growing up? How have things changed since then?

_____

_____

_____

_____

_____

_____

_____

_____

_____

_____

_____

_____

_____

_____

_____

_____

_____

_____

_____

_____

What are some issues you think may come up as you raise your child in a digitally connected world? Where can you go to find advice to help navigate those issues?

_____

_____

_____

_____

_____

_____

_____

_____

_____

_____

_____

_____

_____

_____

_____

_____

_____

_____

When it comes to your child's engagement with technology, what do you hope is true for them 936 weeks from now?

_____

_____

_____

_____

_____

_____

_____

_____

_____

_____

_____

_____

_____

_____

_____

_____

_____

_____

What are your own personal values and disciplines when it comes to leveraging technology? Are there ways you want to improve your own savvy, skill, or responsibility in this area?

_____

_____

_____

_____

_____

_____

_____

_____

_____

_____

_____

_____

_____

_____

_____

_____

_____

_____

Authentic faith

—

TRUSTING JESUS
IN A WAY THAT
TRANSFORMS HOW
I LOVE GOD,
MYSELF,
AND THE REST
OF THE WORLD

THIS YEAR YOU WILL
INCITE WONDER
SO YOUR CHILD WILL KNOW GOD'S LOVE
AND MEET GOD'S FAMILY.

Your baby isn't ready to make a public declaration about what they believe, but that doesn't mean you can't begin to lay a foundation for their faith. In this phase, incorporate faith into a few of your daily routines.

SAY THINGS LIKE . . .

GOD, THANK YOU FOR THIS HEALTHY BABY.
(Pray aloud while you are with your baby.)

JESUS LOVES ME.
(Sing songs while you hold your baby.)

WE ARE GOING TO CHURCH.
(Connect with a faith community.)

Who will help you develop your child's faith as they grow?

_____

_____

_____

_____

_____

_____

_____

_____

_____

_____

_____

_____

_____

_____

_____

_____

_____

_____

_____

_____

_____

_____

_____

_____

_____

_____

Is there a volunteer at your church who shows up consistently each week for your child? Do you attend a consistent service so your baby can begin to feel familiar with the leader who greets them?

_____

_____

_____

_____

_____

_____

_____

_____

_____

_____

_____

_____

_____

_____

_____

_____

_____

When it comes to your child's faith, what do you hope is true for them 936 weeks from now?

_____

_____

_____

_____

_____

_____

_____

_____

_____

_____

_____

_____

_____

_____

_____

_____

_____

_____

_____

_____

_____

_____

What routines or habits do you have in your own life right now that are stretching your faith?

_____

_____

_____

_____

_____

_____

_____

_____

_____

_____

_____

_____

_____

_____

_____

_____

_____

_____

_____

THE

rhythm

OF YOUR

WEEK

—

WILL SHAPE

THE VALUES

IN YOUR

home.

NOW THAT YOU HAVE FILLED THIS BOOK WITH DREAMS, IDEAS, AND GOALS, IT MAY SEEM AS IF YOU WILL NEVER HAVE TIME TO GET IT ALL DONE.

Actually, you have 936 *weeks.*

And every week has potential.

The secret to making the most of this phase with your baby is to take advantage of the time you already have. Create a rhythm to your weeks by leveraging these four times together.

Set the mood for the day.
Smile. Greet them with
words of love.

Reconnect throughout the day.
Make eye contact and
hold them close.

Be personal.
Spend one-on-one time
that communicates love
and affection.

Wind down together.
Provide comfort as the day
draws to a close.

What seem to be your baby's best times of the day?

_____

_____

_____

_____

_____

_____

_____

_____

_____

_____

_____

_____

_____

_____

_____

_____

_____

_____

_____

_____

_____

_____

_____

What are some of your favorite routines with your baby?

_____

_____

_____

_____

_____

_____

_____

_____

_____

_____

_____

_____

_____

_____

_____

_____

_____

_____

_____

_____

_____

Write down any other thoughts or questions you have about parenting your baby.

_____

_____

_____

_____

_____

_____

_____

_____

_____

_____

_____

_____

_____

_____

_____

_____

_____

_____

_____

_____

_____

_____

_____

_____

_____

_____

_____

_____

_____

_____

_____

_____

_____

_____

_____

_____

_____

_____

_____

_____

_____

_____

_____

_____

_____

_____

_____

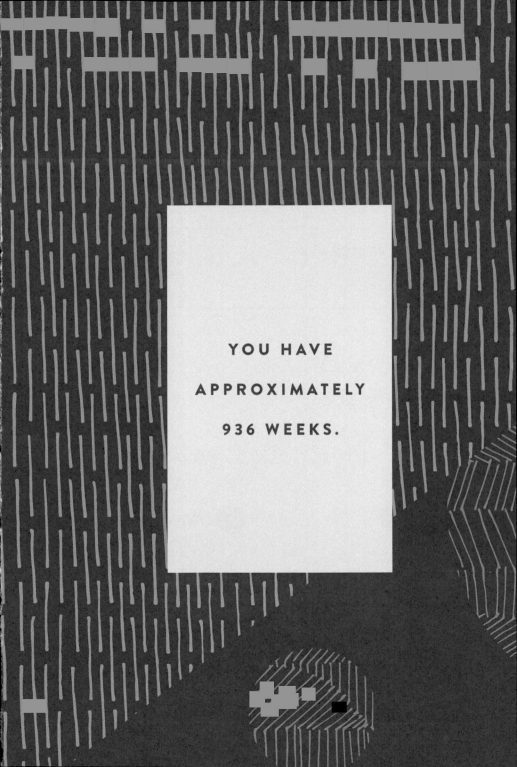

YOU HAVE

APPROXIMATELY

936 WEEKS.

EVERY KID →

MADE I[N]
THE IMA[GE]
OF GO[D]

Incite
wonder

→

SO THEY WILL . . .
KNOW GOD'S LOVE
& MEET GOD'S FAMILY

BEGINNING
(Baby dedication)

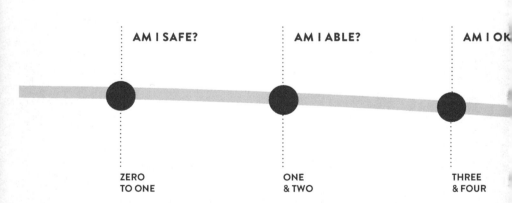

AM I SAFE?

AM I ABLE?

AM I OK[?]

ZERO
TO ONE

ONE
& TWO

THREE
& FOUR

EMBRACE *their physical needs*

TO LOVE GOD

Provoke
discovery $\longrightarrow$ **SO THEY WILL . . .**
TRUST GOD'S CHARACTER
& EXPERIENCE GOD'S FAMILY

 WISDOM
(First day of school)

 FAITH
(Trust Jesus)

AY?

DO I HAVE YOUR ATTENTION?	DO I HAVE WHAT IT TAKES?	DO I HAVE FRIENDS?

K & FIRST · SECOND & THIRD · FOURTH & FIFTH

ENGAGE **their interests**

IT'S JUST
A PHASE
SO DON'T
MISS IT.

ND
-

trust Jesus → TO HAVE A BETTER FUTURE

Fuel
passion  → SO THEY WILL . . .
KEEP PURSUING AUTHENTIC FAITH
& DISCOVER A PERSONAL MISSION

 **FREEDOM**
(Driver's license)

 GRADUATION
(Moving on)

ERE DO I
ONG?

**WHY
SHOULD I
BELIEVE?**

**HOW CAN I
MATTER?**

**WHAT WILL I
DO?**

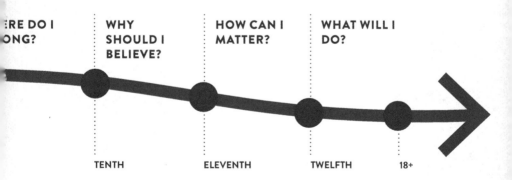

TENTH   ELEVENTH   TWELFTH   18+

MOBILIZE their potential

WITH
ALL THEIR

 HEART

 SOUL

 STRENGTH

A

Provoke

discovery $\longrightarrow$ SO THEY WILL . . .
OWN THEIR OWN FAITH
& VALUE A FAITH COMMUNITY

 **IDENTITY**
(Coming of age)

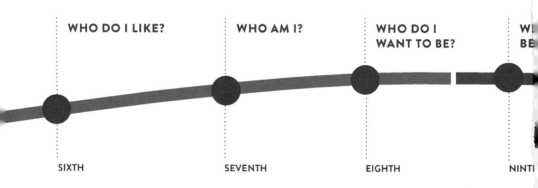

WHO DO I LIKE?   WHO AM I?   WHO DO I
WANT TO BE?   W
BE

SIXTH   SEVENTH   EIGHTH   NINTH

//////// **AFFIRM** their personal journey ////////

ABOUT THE AUTHORS

KRISTEN IVY @kristen_ivy

Kristen Ivy is executive director of the Phase Project. She and her husband, Matt, are in the preschool and elementary phases with three kids: Sawyer, Hensley, and Raleigh.

Kristen earned her Bachelors of Education from Baylor University in 2004 and received a Master of Divinity from Mercer University in 2009. She worked in the public school system as a high school biology and English teacher, where she learned firsthand the importance of influencing the next generation.

Kristen is also the executive director of messaging at Orange and has played an integral role in the development of the elementary, middle school, and high school curriculum and has shared her experiences at speaking events across the country. She is the co-author of *Playing for Keeps*, *Creating a Lead Small Culture*, *It's Just a Phase*, and *Don't Miss It*.

REGGIE JOINER @reggiejoiner

Reggie Joiner is founder and CEO of the reThink Group and co-founder of the Phase Project. He and his wife, Debbie, have reared four kids into adulthood. They now also have two grandchildren.

The reThink Group (also known as Orange) is a non-profit organization whose purpose is to influence those who influence the next generation. Orange provides resources and training for churches and organizations that create environments for parents, kids, and teenagers.

Before starting the reThink Group in 2006, Reggie was one of the founders of North Point Community Church. During his 11 years with Andy Stanley, Reggie was the executive director of family ministry, where he developed a new concept for relevant ministry to children, teenagers, and married adults. Reggie has authored and co-authored more than 10 books including: *Think Orange, Seven Practices of Effective Ministry, Parenting Beyond Your Capacity, Playing for Keeps, Lead Small, Creating a Lead Small Culture*, and his latest, *A New Kind of Leader* and *Don't Miss It*.

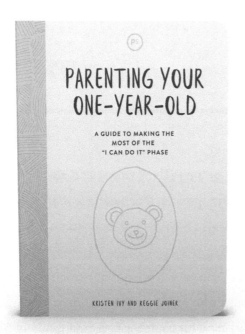

MAKE THE MOST OF EVERY PHASE IN YOUR CHILD'S LIFE

The guide in your hand is one of an eighteen-part series.

So, unless you've figured out a way to freeze time and keep your new baby from turning into a one-year-old, you might want to check out the next guide in this set.

Designed in partnership with Parent Cue, each guide will help you rediscover . . .

**what's changing about your kid,
the 6 things your kid needs most,
and 4 conversations to have each year.**

WANT TO GIFT A FRIEND WITH ALL 18 GUIDES
OR HAVE ALL THE GUIDES ON HAND FOR YOURSELF?

ORDER THE ENTIRE SERIES OF PHASE GUIDES TODAY.